WOF OUTSIDE THE MUSIC BOX

WORSHIP OUTSIDE THE MUSIC BOX

Theology *of* Music & Worship
and Multi-Ethnic Ministry

Stephen Michael Newby

REDEMPTION
PRESS

Published by Redemption Press, PO Box 427, Enumclaw, WA 98022 Toll Free (844) 2REDEEM (273-3336)

Redemption Press is honored to present this title in partnership with the author. The views expressed or implied in this work are those of the author. Redemption Press provides our imprint seal representing design excellence, creative content and high quality production.

ISBN 13: 978-1-63232-095-7 (Print)
          978-1-63232-108-4 (ePub)
          978-1-63232-121-3 (Mobi)
Library of Congress Catalog Card Number: 2015933747

DEDICATION

Dedicated to my wife and son
Stephanie and Silas

CONTENTS

CHAPTER 1

OVERTURE: HOW DO YOU WORSHIP OUTSIDE THE MUSIC BOX?

The first century church was ethnically diverse. Many Jews and Gentiles decided to work together for the advancement of God's kingdom. They worshipped Jesus Christ in a way that blended their cultural preferences so as to become united. In the twenty-first century, as more multiethnic congregations begin to emerge, more friction will ensue in the arena of worship styles, musical genres, and preferred liturgical design. God's people are to gather together to glorify our God. Our personal preferences working in us such as how we might worship God should not be our primary concern. As Christians who worship the triune God, we might consider learning how to gather to worship God in such a way that we actually get along with each other by learning how to momentarily set aside our personal preferences to worship. In doing so, we acquire a greater appreciation for each other's way of worshipping God as we continue to learn about each person's differences, gifts, and what the other person values, likes, and dislikes.

This process of discovering more about what the other person enjoys is a way of looking inside of someone else's life. Each person has a litany of values and biases that defines and qualifies their personal preferences. Appreciating how the other person worships Jesus Christ is a way we look into their style of worship. All Christians have a style of worship that contains a "music box" filled with music of their particular choosing. This music box holds within it a host of robust articulations, presenting and preserving particular musical genres of expressions. Our love, adoration, and worship for God are casted through these expressions. As an important means of pursuing and worshipping God, we are to worship God in community. As a means of worship expression, our worshipping-God communities bring a vast array of music boxes for consideration to use as means of worshipping. Here is the rub: unless there are highly intentional theological, biblical, and spiritual efforts to enjoin these multiple styles, many different musical or worship styles or patterns do not necessarily work well together. Without intentionally working with our worship preferences from the inside of our hearts to the outside of our comfort zones, we might fail to worship as an ingathered reconciled people of God. In order to have great success with multiethnic worship, it is necessary to work strategically outside our music boxes so as to pursue multiethnic worship genres that glorify God.

This book will examine and discuss various theological, philosophical, and artistic constructs based upon the praxis of the interdependence and leading of God's Spirit towards the advancement of multiethnic worship genres in the context of our worship gatherings.

God does not confine the Holy Spirit to a particular style of worship. As humans, by our very nature we are physically confined to reside in these bodies. We are limited with our mortality. Although our humanity limits us physically, God gives us, through the power of the Holy Spirit, power to live in holiness without limits to glorify God. Through

God's holiness there are no limits to what God can do through humanity for God's glory. God's blueprint for humanity is that we live in holiness and wholeness, glorifying Jesus Christ. Should we be living outside of this world's purview? We are charged to live in the world, yet not to be of it. Our true selves are held in these bodies. What we see on the outside is not really the whole of who we are. God calls us to be holy so we should see holiness activities in the world. We should not practice any form of unrighteous prejudice. Our moral compass charges, changes, and challenges our spiritual beings towards holiness as unto the Lord Jesus Christ. God changes us to be more like Jesus Christ. The Holy Spirit changes us. We do not change ourselves. We do not have the capacity to change ourselves. It is through worship that God challenges us to change. We pursue God through worship. Worshipping the triune God changes us. We pursue other forms of Christian worship to humble ourselves unto God. God's creation is vastly filled with the verities, vicissitudes, and reminders of God's grace and provision toward us. Might we have this same grace toward all humanity? We worship God in our comfort zones and from out of them as well. We worship God with other cultures. Every time zone is filled with God's people worshipping God at particular times, same times, different times, and with a varied degree of distinctions and dignities. Although, there are times when our worship can become idolatry. More than likely, those are the times we ought to humble ourselves and not get so caught up into how our worship might be sophisticated, on point, doctrinally sound, multiethnic, or homogenously engaging. Although we aim to be these things, we should be living outside of this world's agenda.

The world has its way of doing things. God has a way of doing things too. The world's agenda has this music box that is filled with all the ideologies of the world. God gives to humanity opportunities to choose what to put in those music boxes. Because God is the grand, wise Creator, God wants us to be creative. We are created in God's image, reflecting the image of God. We are creative beings because God creates. Yet, there are times when our creative nature becomes stagnant, sequestered, spoiled, and soiled in silos. Silos are enclosed containments. That same creative nature funds how we express our worship to God. Our worship articulations must continue to grow and flourish. We should embrace different, creative ways and notions of constant studying and stewarding biblical, theological, and spiritual formation. Within this process of studying, we grow. When we grow, we come out of our comfort zones; we actually come outside of our music boxes.

CHAPTER 2

GOD'S DESIGN, MUSICAL CREED, AND CREATIVITY IS OUT OF THE MUSIC BOX

t is God's design for us to see and experience the styles of many—to come outside of our music boxes. When we see our God worshipped in the heart language of someone else, we are humbled. Realizing that we might not have the ability or capacity to say, "God, I love you, and I worship you" in another's heart language is the first step towards worshipping outside your music box. We humbly realize that we have much to learn from each other and moreover, much to learn from God. The fact of the matter is, that in worshipping God with our wonderful, devout patterns of worship, we sometimes come to particular conclusions that we have figured out how to worship God well.

Perhaps, one might think that the style of multiethnic worship might fall in the same category of inclusionary or exclusionary presuppositions—simply stating—we know how to do this, therefore we are doing it right. But what happens when diverse worship styles are lifted up to God in counterpoint? When this happens, something new and different gives rise. The Holy Spirit who teaches us all things, creates something new that has not been created or experienced before. There will always be something new on God's horizon for God's people. Therefore, God's plan for *diversity design* leads to holiness because God's people are experiencing a wholeness that is only found when the body of Christ is together. This is why the *new song* is sung in Revelation 5. It is sung anew when those who are redeemed sing with many tongues, nations, and kindred. We do multiethnic worship arts ministry because we see it in the Bible. We must always anticipate learning something new from God daily as He gives us our daily bread.

We sing what we believe! If we believe these things to be true, how do we connect our belief with our behavior? Connecting belief and behavior must be practiced. As we read and hear God's Word, we must respond to it. Musically—what we read and hear—we must act accordingly. Music inspires us to respond. One can participate in the discipline of music simply by listening to it. Some people think they are not musicians because they do not play an instrument or sing professionally or semiprofessionally. If you activate some sort of musical apparatus, which plays, performs, or executes sound from any source, you are involved in the process of making music. Dance bands and DJs play music through sound sources. These sound sources impact our hearing. Laypeople make decisions what music they listen to. Laypeople create playlists reflecting diversity, constancy, and consistency of excellence. We make artistic choices every day. We choose to listen to excellent music. We listen to ideas in which we believe. We like to affirm that which we believe. The music to which we listen shapes and gives frame to that which we value. Therefore, in order to validate our point further, we need to explain a dynamic of discipleship in musical terms.

We know the study of music embodies particular constructs of spiritual disciplines and theological notions. Musical terms such as rhythm, melody, harmony, counterpoint, beats, rests, and measures are terms that describe various entities of music. In order for music to be music, it must have these entities present.

Various multiethnic/multi-cross-cultural nuances are necessary for practicing multicultural Christian worship arts. If these elements are not held in high esteem and regard, then the discipline and exploration of multiethnic worship arts will not come to fruition. Music is a great discipline to teach elements or codes of multiethnic leadership ethics and here is why: musicians learn how to work together. They listen to each other. Sometimes for the good of the whole, musicians relinquish their ways of interpreting a piece of music. For the betterment of the group, performing and playing correct harmonies, melodies, counterpoint, timing, and performing in sync are more important than individual artistry and independent imaginative considerations.

For the musical community, playing as a whole unit is imperative. A good music conductor guides and cues the ensemble without attempting to control it. Great musical conductors think about shaping phrases and encouraging dynamics. They think about the design and contour of the music rather than controlling the music. They think about shaping a piece of music rather than shifting or changing that music's purpose into something other than what it is supposed to be. Good musical conductors lead with a multiplicity of diverse skill sets. They spend enormous amounts of time studying and working with each section of the musical community.

Musical conductors are leaders who immerse themselves in the knowledge of all the instruments, their artistic possibilities, and how each musical combination impacts and relates to each other. This is critical. Effective multiethnic leadership groups think about shaping ideas, which give rise in the community. This leadership genre encourages innovation and creative dynamics within the community. This leadership style thinks about the design and contour of community, rather than controlling it. Good, effective multiethnic leadership leads with a multiplicity of diverse skill sets. These skill sets can only be developed through a constancy and diversity of consistent interactions and living with diverse people. These leaders think about encouraging the community to lead collectively by embracing God's design, rather than shifting or changing its purposes into something other than what they are supposed to be. Multiethnic leadership spends enormous amounts of time studying and working with diverse communities. Diverse, multiethnic, pastoral leadership people who immerse themselves in the knowledge of God's Word, God's diverse kingdom, God's diverse church, and the Holy Spirit, will enhance and heighten their awareness and the spiritual possibilities therein. By doing this, they will also learn how God's agenda for us is to live peaceably and fully into holiness and righteous community. We learn how to worship God outside our music box.

The performativity of music unites our humanness to God. Our human physiology works together with soul and spirit to create sound. The mind illumines with imagination and thoughtfulness a particular creativity. Moreover, God's Spirit forms within us, an energy partnering with God in the creative performativity which music brings. Within us we have the God given ability to be partners with God in the creation of music. But we must make the decision to join God in the work.

This God-work is not easy. It is a work of deep discipline, tying together belief and behavior. It is challenging to create something that you have not the experience or narrative to fund accordingly. Within the realm of music, the compositional processes are of the highest spiritual discipline. This process of creating music and holy engagement with God, excites, ignites, and instantiates spiritual verities, pressing into the very marrow of our bones and consciousness of our existence. We sing that which we believe. We sing that which we have become. And we will continue to sing that which we will be forever.

When music motivates us to respond to God, we must believe the music helps us to be free to embrace that which we sing about. When our hearts, minds, and spirits are open to believe in God, God music deliberately liberates in us a performativity to His action. Music moves us—literally and physically. God's musical creed is based upon a love for all creation that is out of the music box. God's music cannot be contained within boundaries of the universe. God's musical work is everlasting. When God's words are pressed into God's music, whatever the musical genre, the music is reconciling, bringing glory to God. What we fail to realize is that no matter how humanly advanced or sophisticatedly inspired our musicality might be, appear to be, or to have become, this music will never be greater than its wise Creator. The music ought to lead us to God and never distract us towards idolatry. Our prayer might be, "Oh Holy Jesus Christ, take hold of our ears, eyes, and heart affections. Let us never leave you for another." The music in our liturgies should draw, bind, and bond us to God. When we sing, "Draw me nearer precious Lord," the rhythm, melodies, harmonies, tempo, metrical articulation (meter, bar lines, phrases, etc.), and counterpoint must work its work to that end. The musical elements should work to do that which we are singing about into our humanity.

The physicality in our humanity frees us to sing. We sing, therefore, we believe, and we become about that which sing. Congregational singing should pull us out of an ordinary gathering into a holy extraordinary engagement with God, serving Him in spirit and in truth.

The Nicene Creed

We believe in one, holy, catholic, and apostolic church. We acknowledge one baptism for the forgiveness of sins. We look for the resurrection of the dead, and the life of the world to come. Amen.

One holy, catholic, and apostolic church has been our creed since its formation in AD 325 at the Nicene Council. This council established its position based upon several criterions, namely Scripture, being one of its funding agencies. Our understanding of this development is shaped and framed through the Scriptures. We are of one faith (vs. heretics), such as to proclaim Christ as our redeemer. We are holy, such as whole, being that we are called out and sanctified to glorify our triune God. We are catholic. We are universal, intergenerational, and multiethnic, representing God's people from all ages and ages to come. We are apostolic. We are communal people living together, worshipping God together, and serving as the hands and feet of Jesus Christ, bringing God's kingdom to earth as it is in heaven. We believe in the forgiveness of sin. This forgiveness is beyond our on capacities. Our assurance in God extends beyond this world. It is existential, pointing to a way forward that is set up for us in the heavenly places. Our belief is in God. Our systems of belief are eschatological. We believe in the world to come, and that our resurrected bodies will be joined with our souls and spirits in that great day of redemption. Finally, we confirm these things with a heartfelt admiration—so be it! Where there is no belief, there is no faith and no purpose for living life on this side of eternity. Following our global

Christian heritage as we did in the first century church, we devote ourselves to God's teaching and fellowship.

> They devoted themselves to the apostles' teaching and to fellowship, to the breaking of bread and to prayer. Everyone was filled with awe at the many wonders and signs performed by the apostles. All the believers were together and had everything in common. They sold property and possessions to give to anyone who had need. Every day they continued to meet together in the temple courts. They broke bread in their homes and ate together with glad and sincere hearts, praising God and enjoying the favor of all the people. And the Lord added to their number daily those who were being saved.
>
> (Acts 2:42–47 ESV)

We, as the first century Christians, commit to serving the poor and those who are without spiritual means. We sacrifice to give God glory and to build God's church. We testify to the power of the resurrection and support the ministry with our prayers and through the physical means, which God has so graciously given to us.

Now the whole group of those who believed were of one heart and soul, and no one claimed private ownership of any possessions, but everything they owned was held in common. With great power the apostles gave their testimony to the resurrection of the Lord Jesus, and great grace was upon them all. There was not a needy person among them, for as many as owned land or houses sold them and brought the proceeds of what was sold. They laid it at the apostles' feet, and it was distributed to each as any had need.

(Acts 4:32–35 NRSV)

Since the genesis of the church, the Holy Spirit has worked beyond our wildest inclinations. Where there has been injustice, holiness and righteousness speak truth to those injustices. The church has stood upon the Nicene Creed through innovative means. Through various trials, tribulations, trails, and tributaries, she has marked her influence and articulated her belief through diverse voices. In the twentieth century, black liberationist theologian, James Cone in his work entitled, *God of the Oppressed*, speaks with ecclesiological nuances to humanity's experiences, asserting there is a basis for speaking universally, traditionally, communally, and holistically through implementations of reconciliation. Part and parcel to a universal church ethos and through *black experience, Scripture,* and *Jesus Christ,* he states:

> The importance of Scripture as the witness to Jesus Christ does not mean that black theology can therefore ignore the tradition and history of Western Christianity. It only means that our study of that tradition must be done in the light of the Truth disclosed in Scripture as interpreted by black people. Although we recognize the interrelationship of Scripture and tradition, especially in the early centuries of the church, yet the full meaning of Scripture is not limited to the interpretation of it as given in that particular tradition.[1]

Cone is thinking across cultural lines. His creedal sensibilities posit his cultural context to a challenge. Furthermore, he states: "I admit readily that the social context of my existence plays an important role in my understanding of the gospel message. However, it would be ridiculous to claim that there is some secret language by which Africans could be persuaded by what I say while non-Africans could never understand it. Clearly there is a basis for speaking across cultural lines, namely, the Bible."[2]

Another diverse voice speaks to the universality of the church. Alexander Schmemann (1921–1983) was an influential Russian Orthodox theologian. He speaks to the reality of the church. He states: "The church, in other terms, is not an 'essence' or 'being' distinct, as such, from God, man, and the world, but is the very reality of Christ in us and us in Christ, a new mode of God's presence and action in His creation, of creation's life in God." Furthermore, He declares, "This world, by rejecting and condemning Christ, has condemned itself; no one, therefore, can enter the Kingdom without in a real sense dying to the world, i.e. rejecting it in its self-sufficiency, without putting all faith, hope, and love in the 'age to come,' in the 'day without evening' which will dawn at the end of time."[3] You are dead and your life is hid with Christ in God" (Col. 3:3). This means that although the church abides in the world, her real life is a constant expectation and anticipation of the world to come, a preparation for it, a passage into reality which in this world can be experienced only as future, as promise and token of things yet to come."[4] We are mystery and yet obvious. "It is the mystery of the church as new creation in its two dimensions—cosmic and eschatological—that reveals to us the meaning and structure of the church as institution."[5] We are one church with many parts. "In this world, the one, holy, catholic, and apostolic church manifests itself as a plurality of churches, each one of which is both a part and a whole."[6] Finally, we are set aside, a sacrament of unity prepared for the age to come. "The church—her identity and continuity with the one, holy, catholic, and apostolic church—is to be the teacher of the universal traditions and the offerer of the Eucharist which is the sacrament of unity."[7] The church has many voices speaking to its unity. We are holy people. We are communal and are people who forgive. We forgive as we have been forgiven of God. We believe in the life everlasting and live as signposts of the new world to come. We live these truths with conviction and commitment. We are the body of Jesus Christ. Therefore, we believe, through faith in Christ Jesus that our ecclesiological formation is ecumenically and eschatologically all encompassing. Ultimately, we will have become what the Holy Father has called us to be—united.

CHAPTER 3

MULTIETHNIC THEOLOGY AND ETHNOCENTRISM

L et's explore how our diverse worship gatherings reflect our unity in Jesus Christ. We see that multiethnic theology is found within the New Testament. God's church is multiethnic. And, because God's church is multiethnic, we must begin to look at this concept as being our identity as God's body. Perhaps, when the church fully embraces the notion of multiethnic ministry the term will become obsolete. As we learn to stand in solidarity with Christians of other ethnicities, we show the world we are Christians by our love for one another. What does that look like at your Sunday morning worship gatherings? Perhaps the majority of North American faith communities have plenty of work to do. As we examine and define multiethnic theology, we must take a serious look again at what God's Word and theologians call the incarnation of Christ and how it relates and points to our homogenous inclinations and our multiethnic sensibilities.

The entire New Testament shows us how first century Jews systematically addressed their relationships with Gentiles. Since we see the life of Jesus Christ as fully human and fully divine, we examine our own natures, cultural contexts, and calling to be one as we are diverse and unified in Christ. We are fully homogenous within our particular species, and we are fully multiethnic within our design for God's kingdom. How do we express our unique homogenous cultural contexts without dumbing down the notion of being unified in Christ as His multiethnic body? This is a critical question.

Culture is important to Jesus Christ. Jesus Christ was Jewish. Cultural identity is the makeup of the multiethnic rendering that God desires for His church.

As the study of Christology is significant to one's faith, understanding, and advancement in God's kingdom, the study of a theology of multiethnic context is critically necessary to a greater understanding of our unity in Jesus Christ.

Ephesians 4:4–6 states there are seven unities to which we must aspire. "There is one body and one Spirit, even as ye are called in one hope of your calling; One Lord, one faith, one baptism, One God and Father of all, who is above all, and through all, and in you all." God's Word proves that within our spiritual DNA, we are to be unified as a multiethnic body of believers. Ephesians 4 points to our unity in Christ. Therefore, our spiritual DNA should reflect that unity all the more.

But verse 7 critically poses how we are to import a patient, longsuffering spirit, and grace-filled essence when we deal with our oneness in Christ Jesus. It states: "But unto every one of us is given grace according to the measure of the gift of Christ." Christians have been given a particular measure of grace to fulfill the seven unities. What is your measure of gift from God? How are you to assert God's biblical unity within your cultural context? Are you grace-filled and longsuffering with others? Are you able to extend grace to others as God extends grace to you?

Why Are the Worship Arts So Important to Multiethnic Theology?

Within its own context, worship arts are diverse. Worship arts hold within them, diverse ways of communicating God's truth. God's truth must be measured and imported within all creation. All our human senses are captured in worship arts. The multiplicity of worship arts reflects a trinitarian doctrine. Where two or three are gathered in God's name, God is present. As we use art to worship God, our motives and intentions are Holy Spirit casted and driven, and the use of multiple art forms honors God. These multiple artistic renderings mirror how Jesus Christ will reconcile and bring together all things. All art can model God reconciling all things. When we gather under the auspices of the Holy Spirit, the Holy Father and Jesus Christ, we worship the triune God.

Worship arts are critical to our multiethnic theology because worship arts espouse within *its characteristics*, practices for necessitating processes of embracing diverse tools for living out holiness and unity with others. Hence, worship arts are multiethnic. Worship arts reflect God's creation. Worship arts allow us to think about our neighbor. In essence, worship arts' essentials are based upon this idea: *Art is about people, but worship is about God.*

When we look at the art of other cultures, we can see with greater clarity God's kingdom reigning in and through humanity. Through the grace and peace of Jesus Christ, worship arts gather us to others. As Jesus Christ will reconcile all things (Col. 3), embracing worship arts is that process by which we can model, right now, what we have not yet apprehended through Christ Jesus.

Who is your *other*? What is an *other*? Is the *other* necessary to our spiritual growth in Christ? We need each other to grow in Christ.

How we can theologically connect how Jesus Christ's incarnation serves as a model for our awareness of serving others? Simply put, Christ came to serve and not to be served, but to give His life to others (Mark 10). Our worship gatherings can reflect this theology of incarnation by simply taking the time to be in the presence of others. God is everywhere and God is with others. Jesus Christ, through the incarnation, came from heaven to earth, crossed the cultural comfort zone within the heavens to become human and to live out the one and true example for us. This idea of crossing the cultural comfort zone is explored on earth when we gather with a theology of righteous, multiethnic diversity.

Now that we can theologically connect how Jesus Christ's incarnation models for our personal otherness, we might be able to see how necessary our otherness is for us to become like Christ. Our *otherness* is not about us. It is about how we relate to *others*. Otherness is about others. Otherness is about *those people over there*.

Otherness is about how we deal those people over there who actually have nothing to do with us because of our indifference or because of our radical, hidden, selfish, and intense tendencies and intentions to ignore, cast aside, or with prejudice become compassionless towards those others. How do we radically expose this form of idolatry? Being with others radically exposes our weaknesses and forms of idolatry.

If our Christian worship gatherings are to shape and form us in the image of Christ, then our gatherings must be diverse. God's people are diverse and our gatherings should be also. There is absolutely no excuse for Christian North Americans not to embrace these truths. We who live in the free world must articulate our freedom and liberty in Christ through our gatherings so that the world will know we are Christians by our love.

When diverse arts work in concert together, they reflect how God's people ought to worship God together.

Blended worship functions as a bridge to fund our reality as God's body. It is a well-funded bridge. The idea of blended worship helps us to invent.[1] The idea of inventing serves innovation. Innovation leads us to invitation. Blended worship is nothing more than an invitation to examine other options for Christian worship. Once the invitation is received, there are greater considerations for being transformed as a community that will reflect the diversity within God's kingdom. Only the Holy Spirit can radically teach us how to become innovative. Since God is creating all things new, God is the author and finisher of innovation. We can only innovate when we seek God and ask God for innovation. The gift of innovation is a perfect gift from the Father above. God the Father, through Jesus Christ, will reconcile all innovation.

Worship Arts are collaborative in nature. When we collaborate we innovate. Perhaps some of our most creative innovations emerge from collaboration. God said, "Let us make man in our image"

(Gen. 1:26). This is the example of innovation from collaboration.

As Blended Worship Is a Creative Mixture of Old and New, Multiethnic Gatherings Are a Mixture of Many Artistic Entities.

As a movement, blended worship prepared our hearts for change in the church. For we who hold to a North American ecclesiology, will find the New Testament church is already blended, multiethnic, diverse, and with our own particular *ethnocentrisms.*[2]

> But ethnocentrism should not be worshiped. Nothing in the world is to be worshiped. The doctrine of creation is a great warning and battle cry against all forms of idolatry. Idolatry is by definition giving absolute loyalty to something that is only a creature rather than to the Creator. When the good gifts of God are made substitutes for God, they become demonic, enslaving, and destroying even as they promise to help, fulfill, and save. We see how this happens when we think of the gods modern people worship as absurdly as ancient people worshiped images of woods or gold.[3]

Let us consider the idea of worshiping how we worship God. Is it possible that forms of worship can become idolatry? One might argue if that is the case, then diverse worship elements or multiethnic worship as a style within itself, can become idolatry. This statement is true. However, the inclinations toward idolatry might be much more insidiously founded and deeply embedded within ethnocentrism, homogenous gatherings, and ways of doing and embracing the styles therein. People love being with their own kind. Who does not like being with people who look like them, enjoy the same types of things, and speak the same language, especially the same worship language? When it is all said and done, people easily get along well with others who are like them.

Multiethnic Gatherings Enable Us to Experience a Tension so as to Teach and Admonish One Another in the Ways of Jesus Christ.

Remember the Colossians 3:16 passage where it states: "Let the Word of Christ dwell in you richly, teaching and admonishing one another in psalms, hymns and spiritual songs ..." Is it possible while we immerse ourselves in God's Word and sing through diverse musical genres,

God's Word is richly shaping us to be unified as God's body while we learn to sing God's truth through various styles, languages, beats, meters, rhythms, melodic shapes, and musical sounds? Yes, because the discipline of music allows us to physically and holistically reflect and nuance the depth, breadth, height, and length of that which we are to become in Jesus Christ. Diverse worship gatherings reflect our unity in Jesus Christ. When diverse people come together, tension is created. That tension will either pull our attention towards that tension or draw us to the cross of Jesus Christ. Perhaps we might choose to be selfish, losing our way towards a unity in Christ. We head towards idolatry, and this process reveals how much more God's spirit and truth is to give rise in our lives, and our idolatry is exposed. Ethnocentrism can be driven by sin or it can be used by God to drive sin out of us. We will either use our ethnicity as a tool to bring glory to God or not. Our ethnicity is beautiful. God created His creations and creatures with a particular identity. That identity is casted into an ethnicity. But our primary identity is borne through God. We are made in the image of the all-knowing and wise Creator.

God's creation and creatures have been and always will be diversely expressing and articulating a particular ethnicity. Where there is no holy diversity, there is no possibility for a holy unity in Christ. We in this twenty-first century have technological advances and liberties to follow through on God's mandate for unity. We can pray with others who are near and far within a moment's notice. We can gather sophisticatedly with visual aids to help us clarify our diversity in Christ Jesus. If we choose to embrace this essential means of holiness unto the Lord, we can embrace the healthy, holistic, radical, reconciling love for God's multiethnic New Testament church. Loving others with the love of the Lord glorifies God, shines God's light in our darkened world, and testifies to the Father's good work through us (Matt. 6). Through Jesus Christ and His model of the incarnation, we can righteously and systematically address our relationships with others, giving glory to heavenly Father, Jesus Christ, and the Holy Spirit. We are an extension of the New Testament's first century Jewish inquiry. Our diversity reflects God's kingdom coming to earth, God's will being done on earth as it is in heaven, and our willingness to die to our personal biases, selfish motivations, sins of omission and commission, as well as a host of other various forms of spiritual distractions. The art of worship is ultimately manifested within the notion of what we are willing to sacrificially give up, such as to glorify God. When we worship God we give of ourselves. We relinquish those things that hold us back from giving God our all. When our worship attracts us to Christ, our lives will attract others to Christ too.

CHAPTER 4

THE HOLY SPIRIT CHANGES US, CHANGE IS MULTICULTURAL

Culture is filled with change. Many diverse cultures challenge us to change. Hence, change challenges us to change. We change. We grow. We diminish. We thrive. On one hand, we might not see change coming towards us and miss it. On the other hand, change does not miss us. Change can hit us like a ton of bricks. Sometimes it catches us off guard. Other times we can anticipate change and brace ourselves to embrace it.

Cultures change. People change. Leadership changes. Churches change. Congregations can be challenged by change. Change is constant, and time changes everything. Time matters to God. Change matters to God. God wants us to mature and grow in grace and in the knowledge of God. Most of the time we fight change. God has a formula and prescription to change us. Change should be a primary function for God's people! Yes, to appreciate our changing within creation, we must abide and find our abode with the *Holy Spirit*. What is the Holy Spirit doing? The Holy Spirit is changing us! Perhaps in order for the North American church to have a greater impact worldwide, she must consider changing her appearance from primarily homogenous and become multicultural deeply within her leadership.

When a homogenous congregation is in the midst of change or transition, can that church envision a leadership before them that represents a multicultural sensibility without compromising a righteous holiness as unto the Lord? Could a black, homogenous congregation have a Hispanic or French senior pastor? Could a dominant-culture congregation submit to a non-dominant senior pastoral leadership? In your ministry, what does the art of submission to the Spirit of God look like? Are we allowing people to operate in their gifting? Do we practice particular prejudices without realizing it? Might a senior pastor consider serving as the custodian for two weeks? Perhaps in some congregations that is already taking place. Is the size of a congregation so small that the senior pastor does everything? Then perhaps why not allow laypeople to deliver homilies or short sermons? What does the Bible say about these issues? Change is multicultural. How might our church leadership's sensibilities reflect a God-centered holiness, which is found in a diverse, doctrinally sound, biblical, theological, spiritual, imaginative, and multicultural leadership without compromising our moral compass as unto the Lord? God's Spirit teaches us how to accomplish this task (Rom 12).

God's Spirit Works Multiculturally with the Local Body

Are we spending time seeking God's Spirit? Are we wasting time by not seeking the Spirit? Why waste time? Wasting time is idolatry. But the general presupposition lies in the matter of this question. Why am I doing what I am doing? What are my motivations and intentions? What is God's Spirit saying to us? If we are motived through God Spirit's to inform, fund, and feed our expectations for living for God, then we just focus on God and God's kingdom, right?

What does your church look like? Is it multi-cultural? Presently, I attend Antioch Bible Church in Seattle, Washington. Antioch considers itself a multiethnic church. Antioch has a kingdom of God philosophy of ministry. It is based upon the Seven Purposes of Antioch:

A   All Members Ministering
N   New Testament Model
T   Teaching God's Word
I   Intercession
O   Outreach
C   Cross-Cultural
H   Healthy Worship

With the notion that every area of ministry must import excellence and integrity within, Antioch's ABCs:

A   Attitude towards Worship
B   Building Intentional Relationships
C   Cross-Cultural Teams

Every area of ministry must prioritize these values: *People* are always first, *programs* are always second and *facilities* are always third. Our motto has been, *we exist by equipping God's people of all cultures and ethnicities, to do the work of the*

*Christian ministry to the world. Antioch Bible Church
exists to glorify God.*

One must be intentional to practice multiethnic
ministry. Intentionality with commitment and
contentment will get the job done. I am learning
how to be content when I am abounded or abased.
I am learning how not to depend on my own
strength and giftedness—whatever that might
be. This awareness is God's grace given to us in
unmeasured favor. God's grace is at the core of
our existence, sustaining us towards a fruitful life.
Praise the Lord!

Intergenerational Worship is Multicultural

How can we continue to create ministry opportunities expressing beliefs and values of equipping
young leaders for our future generations? While
settling in the trenches of ministry, we must continue in not relinquishing or letting go of control.
Consider the importance of allowing young people
to lead in our congregations. The church is not
ours to own. We are to steward it. This is not our
world. "The earth *is* the Lord's and all its fullness,
the world and those who dwell therein" (Ps. 24:1
NKJV). It is only by the power of relating to the next
generation and praying for them that we can help

them to become change agents for God's kingdom. For prayer is everything.[1] Sharing leadership responsibilities with the next generation is critical. As the youth can learn much from the elders, the elders can learn much from the youth. This is why intergenerational worship is important.

And when we pray and sing together, in effect, we actually mirror the hope and good future and peace that God brings to us! Praise the Lord! We pray for leadership that will send our churches flourishing! We pray that God will fill the next generation with the Holy Spirit to enlarge God's territory on earth as it is in heaven.

The Holy Spirit Works Multiculturally in the Global Church

There must be an incredible diversity of theologies of the Holy Spirit—perhaps as many as there are denominations. However, Clark Pinnock's postulations clearly bridge and bring currency to a wide range of perspectives, hence reconciling many thoughts and ideas into one cohesive means of bringing balance to the doctrine of the Holy Spirit. Pinnock posits the notion of Spirit into three categories: *Spirit and union, Spirit and universality* and *Spirit and truth.*

In the order of Spirit and union, Pinnock decrees salvation is diverse, claiming: "Obviously salvation is multifaceted and has many dimensions—conversion, new birth, justification and sanctification—but the goal is surely glorification and union with God."[2] Moreover, "Union with God is a state of intimacy, and sexual imagery may be used for it. Paul says that the love of male and female points to the mystery of Christ's love for us."[3] God is a God of order. One might think God's parental nature, if you will, would be that of a disciplinarian. Furthermore, Pinnock states, "God convicts and moves us toward intimacy."[4] This notion of conviction and relationship is not necessarily a characteristic easily found within humanity's capacity. Within our humanity, conviction impacts how we relate to one another. However with God, that is not the case. For it is God who draws us near. "Spirit may draw, but people must consent. The Spirit helps us, but we are also co-workers with God."[5] We must submit our will to the Spirit's ordering of the day—every day and in every moment. This is the key to a working relationship with God's spirit. Simply stated, "apart from grace there cannot be faith, but faith is authentically a human response and act of cooperation."[6]

Pinnock asserts under the notion of Spirit and universality, that "Spirit is present in the farthest reaches of this wonderful, ambiguous world" and "The cosmic breath of Spirit activities can help us conceptualize the universality of God's grace."[7] Due to the nature of our capacity to discern on our own, our perspectives on redemption and reconciliation are limited. "The scope of redemption is universal, but Scripture suggests that one can be finally impenitent and be excluded from the kingdom" (Rev. 21:8, 27).[8] We have not the capacity to see the future. That is not our business. But we are to live out our lives holistically as unto the Holy Spirit.

Therefore, when we look holistically at God's universe, we should avoid universalism and restrictivism. For it is "*Jesus* Christ, *who* represents particularity by being the only mediator between God and humanity (1 Tim. 2:5–6), while the Spirit upholds universality because no soul is beyond the sphere of the Spirit's operations. The Spirit is not confined to the church but is present everywhere, giving life and creating community."[9]

Finally, Pinnock suggests that, as a category to assert God's Spirit and truth, God enlivens us with the Spirit to provide a witness to the world. "The Spirit makes the truth come alive and provides a witness in the hearts of believers (1 Cor. 2:4, 1 John 2:27)."[10] When we bond with God we see a greater interconnectedness with God's creation and salvific plan for the world. "The Spirit is as the bond of love in the triune relationality, as the ecstasy of sheer life overflowing into a significant creation, as the power of creation and new creation, as the power of incarnation and atonement, as the power of new community and union with God, and as the power drawing the whole world into the truth of Jesus Christ."[11] Pinnock's text allows us to perceive the Holy Spirit's role differently. While examining a theology of the Holy Spirit within these three domains: Spirit and union, Spirit and universality and Spirit and truth, we are encouraged to strive for a spiritual discernment that brings balance and equity to a multitude of interpretations and operations within the Spirit.

Scripture for reflection:

When the Day of Pentecost had fully come, they were all with one accord in one place.

> And suddenly there came a sound from heaven, as of a rushing mighty wind, and it filled the whole house where they were sitting. Then there appeared to them divided tongues, as of fire, and one sat upon each of them. And they were all filled with the Holy Spirit and began to speak with other tongues, as the Spirit gave them utterance.
>
> (Acts 2:1–4)

Holy Writ teaches us to observe all things, quench not the Spirit of God and pray without ceasing (1 Thess. 5:17–19 ESV). Pinnock states: "Just as there has been neglect of the Spirit as Creator, there has been neglect concerning the work of the Spirit in relation to Christ."[12] Hence, a truly and true understanding of Spirit Christology must not be understated. Investigating Christ's relationship with the Spirit, Pinnock states: "It was the anointing by the Spirit that made Jesus Christ, not the hypostatic union, and it was the anointing that made him effective in history as the absolute Savior."[13] And, it is "by the Spirit *that* he has also become through resurrection the first fruits of a new humanity. As a result of his assuming our human nature as last Adam, Jesus has created a new human situation." There is a new creation

(2 Cor. 5:17). As a result, "We all in union with Christ by the power of the Spirit, are enabled to participate in divine life."[14] For "it was by the Spirit that Jesus was conceived, anointed, empowered, commissioned, directed, and raised up."[15]

According to theologian Jeff Keuss, our Christian tradition starts speaking of the Spirit by asserting that the Holy Spirit is God. Back in the days of early church, Athenagoras wrote that the Spirit was an *emanation* of God the Father, and some others thought of the spirit in the same terms as the *Talmudic* discussions on the divine *Shekinah* (Presence) as an expression of what Christians call the Father.[16] The Spirit has the attributes of God: eternal—having neither beginning nor end (Heb. 9:14), omnipotent—having all power (Luke 1:35), omnipresent—being everywhere at the same time (Ps. 139:7), and omniscient—understanding all matters (1 Cor. 2:10–11).[17]

Throughout Holy Writ, we clearly see the Holy Spirit's role as essential. "The Gospels go out of the way to connect Jesus with the Spirit on all kinds of occasions in His life—birth, baptism, temptation, preaching, healing, exorcisms, death and resurrection. Overall, they reveal Jesus as a gift of the Spirit."[18] "Humanity will be restored to *a greater* communion with God. The Spirit is prominent in the birth because it points forward to Pentecost and new creation."[19] Finally, Pinnock decrees: "I realize that *Spirit Christology* might not be the best term to use. Spirit is used by liberals to refer to the divine element in Jesus, not the third person of the Trinity dwelling in him. *Spirit Christology* as used by them refers to an inspirational, not an incarnational, Christology. When I refer to Spirit Christology, I do so in an orthodox way that preserves the trinitarian distinctions. Spirit Christology enriches but does not replace logos Christology."[20]

In early church creeds, little is said about the Holy Spirit. And historically, the church has been unable to fully negotiate her challenges within the traditional understanding of the doctrine of the Holy Spirit. Theologian and author Kathryn Tanner asserts that although our processes of theological inquiry might and can be tainted, God's Spirit, despite ourselves, continues to reveal and teaches us a greater understanding and revelation of ourselves and Christ's work in and through us. Tanner states: "The Spirit is thought to work gradually and without final resolution in and through the usual fully human and fully fallible, often messy and conflict-ridden public processes of give and take in ordinary life."[21] Pinnock affirms and confirms Tanner's position by stating, "The Spirit's work in creation anticipates the work of redemption."[22]

The Holy Spirit acts, moves, gives rise, and energizes. The Spirit is described as God in action. The Holy Spirit is the Spirit of Christ (Gal. 4:6). The Holy Spirit works in people (1 Cor. 6:19), in community (1 Cor. 3:16) and in the world (John 16:8–11). The work of the Spirit is active in the world (Acts 2:11), instilling new life as spiritual rebirth (John 3:3–5) and providing knowledge and guidance (Acts 16:7).[23]

Historically, the church, no doubt, has articulated its multiplicity of interpretations and understandings of the Holy Spirit's role, function, and position in the Trinity. Nonetheless, the Holy Spirit is a full member within the Trinity. "Wherefore I give you to understand, that no man speaking by the Spirit of God calleth Jesus accursed: and *that* no man can say that Jesus is the Lord, but by the Holy Ghost" (1 Cor. 12:3).

When we listen to *other's* stories, we get to know them deeply. I believe an ethnographic disposition as unto the Lord will bring to fruition *trust, truth,* and *transparency.* Therein is a great gift to the church. The challenges lie within the listener. Can one listen and be attentive with a sense of hunger and inquiry? One must listen actively and not passively. One must attune to the language and character of the social context and constructs within that particular community. Learning the tools of active listening, relating to the community with wishful thinking, emancipatory hope, and nourishing action is critical for the way forward as we engage in this extraordinary way of embracing ministry in the twenty-first century.[24] We must listen to the Spirit. The Spirit changes us to be holy. Perhaps for the western church this change is embracing multicultural worship gatherings as well.

CHAPTER 5

JESUS IS MULTICULTURAL, TRINITARIAN LIFE, AND THE SPIRIT CONNECT US TO CHRIST

Participating and Being with Jesus Christ and His Body

It is modeled for us through God's trinitarian essence, as made visible and tangible through the Holy Spirit that we are in relationship with Christ. And this relationship is about our worshipping God. Jesus Christ models this for us in Scripture and Jesus Christ's incarnation is a signpost for multiethnic worship. James Cone states, "The least in America are literally and symbolically present in black people. To say that Christ is black means that black people are God's poor people whom Christ has come to liberate."[1] Furthermore, Kathryn Tanner states, "As adopted

sons we are to enjoy the true divine Son's preroga-
tives, through relations with the other persons of
the trinity in some sense comparable to the ones
that the second person of the trinity has."[2]

"The Spirit would therefore establish Jesus' own
Son-ship in much the same way that a number of
mostly Pauline texts suggest the Spirit establishes
ours. Just as the Spirit makes us Christ's own so
that we may be sons like him, the Spirit makes
Jesus' own humanity that of the Son of God."[3]

Whatever our ethnicity might be and no matter
what we assert about our identity, for Christians
that is, our identity is to be summed up in Jesus
Christ. And there must be something of great value
found within our humanity. Jesus Christ, very
God and very human, suffered for us. Jesus Christ
presents a divinity that cannot be dumbed down
or polluted. Christ is not a fixture of that which
we must become, but overtakes us with His eternal
mediation of transfiguration and transformation.
Simply stated, this is new life—a new way of living.

As theologian James Cone postulates "*Jesus is
Black*," it is more than a simple notion of the hue
of His skin. "The 'blackness of Christ,' therefore, is
not simply a statement about skin color, but rather,
the transcendent affirmation that God has not ever,

no not ever, left the oppressed alone in struggle. He was with them in Pharaoh's Egypt, is with them in America, Africa and Latin America and will come in the end of time to consummate fully their human freedom."[4] This matter is about Jesus Christ being present with those who are exiled, those who live amongst community disarticulation, and those who realize our humanness can be lived out in deep relationship beyond outward appearances.

Therefore, as Christ liberates us from ourselves and places us in relationship to the *trinitarian life*, we are living in exile and living through exhaling the breath of God's kingdom into humanity anew. We live through God's Spirit and God's Word—God's Son. For Jesus says it is not about just rules, but it is about love too. We participate in the "Trinitarian character of human life."[5] We are not formed by rules. What forms us is the way we interact with each other. We give hold to an inheritance given to us in Christ. God the Father presses the God-man in our lives—Jesus touches our lives and restores them. Our lives are always performing something! We are to perform that which we see Jesus doing. We are living into the idea of what a Christian is to do. We are trying to proclaim and navigate—through formation and agency—that life Jesus is living into our humanity. Being human is now being bound into His existence. God does more than restore our lives.[6] Through the life of Christ, His historicity with humanity, and His eternal place with Father and the Holy Spirit, we engage with the rhythms and movements of God's life, with "new organizing principles of human living."[7] God brings to us a justice that is beyond our comprehension. And it is through the Spirit that we are shaped and formed as well. Tanner posits, "Receiving that Spirit, we become like Christ in His relations with the Father. More particularly, the Spirit unites us to Christ in a way that gives us access to the Father and the Father's gifts. The Spirit connects us to Christ.[8] We, God's people, worship God in three persons—the blessed Trinity. Therefore, we practice living a trinitarian life by living peaceably with all people.

This is how we are shaped and transformed— through the Spirit we have power to be first, then we are able, through Jesus Christ, to be the hands and feet of the wise Creator. Because Jesus Christ is the head of a multicultural body, Jesus Christ is multicultural.

CHAPTER 6

MULTICULTURAL LISTENING, PRAYING, AND SINGING WITH JESUS CHRIST AND HIS BODY

While listening to a sermon, most congregates expect to learn something new spiritually, biblically, and theologically. Most congregates do not even think about or consider learning something new when singing familiar hymns or other various forms of sacred song, especially Holy Scripture. Colossians 3 speaks to the idea of singing a new song and teaching each other through diverse art forms. One of the reasons we might consider seeking out a variety of artistic worship genre expressions is to learn how to hear and learn from the Holy Spirit, the heavenly Father, and Jesus Christ differently. We listen to Holy Scripture. We need to order our lives through God's Word. We sing God's Word. We ought to follow God's teaching with a deeper sense of presence because the physicality of the singing Holy Writ changes our entire being. Our whole being sings, therefore our whole being is being submitted to God's will. Bible teachers are expected to make a biblical commentary on the Word, and artists should be teachers who biblically commentate as well. And when we sing God's Word with different music, we make a biblical and musical commentary upon Scripture.

Our commentaries are declarations upon that which we believe. This is sound doctrine with sound. When we import new musical material, keys, tonal centers, meters, rhythms, counterpoint, or expand or contract a known melody of a hymn, we make a spiritual declaration. That declaration is an expansion of a biblical idea. When we rearrange or reconstitute a musical idea we, in effect, articulate the biblical truth of God reconciling all things to God's glory (Col. 1). Since God will reconcile all things through Jesus Christ, is it possible that most artistic presentations will be reconciled if there is a genre of music that previously had been used profanely? Hence, can it be used in a sacred context to give God glory?

The answer is yes—well, not totally yes, yet. Ecclesiology teaches us that God's church has been, is, and will continue to be diverse. The heavenly Father is diversifying the church by populating heaven and depopulating hell. The Holy Spirit is saving, sanctifying, and glorifying the church. Jesus Christ is constantly reconciling and making all things new (Col. 4). God is constantly expanding His kingdom. New populations of humanity are coming to the saving knowledge of Jesus Christ. God's heaven is being populated. Recreating and bringing together diverse people for God's glory is Jesus Christ's reconciliation in action. With Christ as our head, Christ's diverse body is put together so that the world will see the Word of God made flesh with His church, the hands and feet of Jesus Christ, doing the work of God while it is possible to work. Art is continually and constantly, with diversity, being reconciled to God. This art reflects new people groups from generations of diversity. Therefore, we are reconciled but not fully reconciled yet.

God's body is diverse. Therefore, God's body, in order to be healthy, must seek to work well together. Our multicultural listening and hearing helps us to hear the diverse *worship symphony of*

God's song in this present age, which is our calling to fulfill. We must listen to God's body. What is going on with God's people? We cannot selfishly be content when one organ of the body, one area of the body, and/or one section of the body is hurting. God wants to bring healing to His church/His body. So when we practice multicultural listening to the worship styles of many nations, we, in essence, become sensitive and very aware of that group's concerns and cares within that community. When we listen, we pay attention, we pray, we care, and we become like Christ. Christ is listening to diverse prayers and interceding for all the saints. We, too, must be in prayer and supplication for others. When we sing the songs of other nations we in turn are praying with those nations who are reflecting the unity of the Spirit and casting their cares before the Lord. We live out Jesus Christ's prayer in John 17. We are unified and the world sees that we are Christians by our love and concern for all people. Therefore, we listen and participate multiculturally because Jesus Christ is doing the same thing right now, interceding for us. While listening to songs and prayers from people of other cultures, we should expect to learn something new spiritually, biblically, and theologically about God's body and in effect, we grow in grace and in the knowledge of the Lord's will and kingdom agenda.

Christ was Jewish. But, He did not think His Jewishness or Jewish preferences to be one that would override the need to go through Samaria to teach one of the greatest lessons on multiethnic spirit and truth worship in the Bible (John 4). Our worship must be heavenly Father, Jesus Christ, and Holy Spirit centered, not ethnic or multi-genre centered. Genre is about people and worship is about God. Oh that God would give our souls the invitation to worship that is all about relationships glorifying God: living in holiness with diverse communities and living in the tension without bringing attention to personal sacrifice. We therefore, must engage in new worshipping ways with multiethnic sensibilities, paying attention to orthodoxy, holy ecumenicalism, and righteousness which leads to loving mercy, doing justice, and walking humbly before God (Mic. 6).

For some dominant culture theologians and Bible teachers, the presupposition that Christ's skin color is light is more than a notion. Perhaps for some dominant culture North Americans, it probably sounds insulting or ridiculous to say that Jesus Christ is black. But Jesus Christ's humanity is more than a simple notion of the hue of His skin.

Since Jesus Christ is present with us, how might we emulate that reality via our worship gatherings? We must explore these issues with a liberation and freedom that can only be found in the notion of reflecting a *Trinitarian life*, a life in deep relationship with others. The Trinity does this, and so we should too. Genetically, the human race is invariably connected. We celebrate our connectedness because of Jesus Christ. When we proudly lift up our diversity as a theme of focus and great significance outside of Christ's identity, we commit idol worship (Hos. 11). No matter how diverse one's community might become or how great the multiplicities of diversity one can muster up, we, on our own volition, cannot and will never advance God's kingdom agenda without submitting those diversities to the holiness and righteousness of the Holy Trinity. There might be a way that seems right in our own rendering but the end thereof is to our own destruction (Prov. 3). Jesus Christ is the author and finisher of our multiethnic renderings. It is through Christ that we do all things (Phil. 4).

Since we are shaped and transformed by Christ modeling for us how to live by God's Word and the Holy Spirit, the same Word and Spirit of God that is at work in diverse Christian communities all over the world is at work in your community. This simple notion is critical. When we understand that the same God working in other cultures is working in you, we withhold and release presuppositions of entitlement. We should not presuppose that we who appear to hold a greater economic power than other people groups, are more blessed or have greater connection to God. Our heavenly Father is the source through which all other things are resourced (James 2). A multicultural theology of economic ethics is of great importance, so as to take care of the widows, orphans, and those who are destitute. The poor will always be amongst us, and we must take care of those who are without means. Diverse populations include the poor, rich, single, and married people too. If someone is your opposite, then embrace them with a spirit of holiness in diversity and serve them. Serve someone else who cannot possibly reciprocate that which you have given. That is what Jesus Christ has done for us.

Whether We Accept It or Not, the Church Is Multicultural. It Always Has Been and It Always Will Be.

Perhaps we can now begin to explore Christology and incarnation as signposts for multiethnic worship. Jesus Christ is the second

Adam. Christ is relating all the time with His body. The triune God is the greatest example of healthy relationships. The effectiveness and rationality behind relationships and all forms of relating to something or someone is solely based upon the clarity and excellence within communicative processes. There are no communication issues amongst the Trinity.

The Gospel of Saint John begins with a declaration of communication stating and serving as a declaration of beginning of all beginnings. This declaration postulates the centrality of Jesus Christ, while assuming we have a response to that declaration. *"In the beginning was the Word and the Word was with God and the Word was God"* (John 1:1). What do we make of this declaration? This inquiry lays out notions of communication that are subtle. Having been misappropriated through means of familiarity and informality, we know these words communicate, but do we understand that the beginning of all communications becomes possible through and only through Jesus Christ? The connection between all knowledge and all that is and has been created is to be found in Jesus Christ. Christ is the beginning of all communicative processes. For

Jesus Christ as Alpha and the Omega—beginning and end—funds and feeds humanity's existence, awareness, and trajectory. It is only through Jesus Christ that we can live, move, and have our being. It is only through Jesus Christ's incarnation that our existences, awareness, and trajectories have at its core, the knowledge of Christ whose centeredness can only be articulated through communication that might lead to relationships; this is at the center of everything that supports humanity.

Theologian Bonhoeffer states:

> To sum up, we must continue to emphasize that Christ is truly the center of human existence, the center of history and now also the center of nature. But these three aspects can only be distinguished from each other in abstract. In fact, human existence is also and always history, always and also nature. The mediator as fulfiller of the law and liberator of creation is all this for the whole human existence. He is the same who is intercessor and *pro me*, and who is himself the end of the old world and the beginning of the new world of God.[1]

Christ is the center of our human existence. Christ is multicultural, and we should care about multicultural issues. Should we concern ourselves with questions such as: which came first the homogenous church or the multiethnic church? This is the wrong question. We should seek to observe that the Jews were God's chosen people first, and then the Gentiles came upon the scene. God's salvific purview was always for all people (Gal. 3:26–29).

Our first aim is to worship God. Then we are to love our neighbors as we love ourselves. No need to convince ourselves to love ourselves. That is what we really do well. We just need to be convinced that when we love others as we love ourselves we, in fact, are loving on ourselves. We are Christ's body. When a husband mistreats his wife he is sinning against her and himself. Husbands and wives are deeply connected. The body of Christ is deeply connected too. The church is God's body. When it is all said and done, we ought to love others no matter what the circumstances. Loving others does not necessarily mean that we are irresponsible with that love. Loving others well means that we hold to a moral compass that our heavenly Father presents to us. This must be our deep commitment. This must be our deep perspective. This must be our glorying in God. We must be concerned about the needs of others before our own needs

(Phil. 2). Our identity is summed up in Jesus Christ. There must be something of great value found in others. Humanity is important to God and therefore it must be important to us. Simply stated, here in North America, we are loaded with resources so as to serve the entire world. We have created both systems of togetherness and segregation. The church's job is to glorify God by being together. When the head is removed from the body there is death. When the body does not function properly there is sickness. Have you thought that if the church could be connected through the Holy Spirit, technological advances, and a will to create new systems of caring for, protecting, providing for, and serving each other, how might this new system serve a greater visibly connecting God's body? Why would God purposely come to engage with great intentionality the creation that is so easily distracted from its wise Creator? Jesus Christ suffered for us in the flesh. This theme is recapitulated over and over for us throughout God's story. And the whole creation is to be saved upon this essence of incarnation.

Theologian Tanner postulates, "The whole of creation becomes an image of the second person of the trinity in this way: that what came into being might not only be, but be good, it pleased God that His own wisdom should condescend to the creatures, so as to introduce an impress and semblance of its image on all in common and on each, that which was made might be manifestly wise works and worthy of God."[2] The incarnation was an act of obedience for Christ. Since the Son of God was charged to engage with humanity, we too are to engage with humanity. Since by man came death. Since by Christ came life, and that new life is the central theme within Holy Writ. This is good. This is good news. The Word communicates new life, we are to live our new lives, as God's Spirit equips us to live it, seek it, pursue it, to do goodly with it, and speak it. Perhaps only through Christ we will learn to speak, declare, and communicate the excellence of our redeemer King. For after all Jesus is our head and we the body. For the effectiveness of all, our relating with each other and the world must be based upon communicating that Christ is the key, Christ is the center, and our centeredness must dwell within the triune God.

CHAPTER 7

A THEOLOGY OF RELATIONSHIPS, PHILEMON

This epistle teaches us quite a bit about cross-cultural relationships, multiethnic leadership, and cultural contextualized discernment between two homogeneous populations (dominant and non-dominant), i.e. those who have sufficient means and those who are without basic needs for living. Paul opens the letter with the assurance of his status as a prisoner of Jesus Christ. What can we learn from this letter that will shape and form our ethos for living well in diverse Christian communities?

Do you think there are stresses between dominate and non-dominant cultures in North

America? What has Christ modeled for us in Philippians 2 regarding our expectations and entitlements for status in community, and, in Paul's letter to Philemon, what has he asked of him regarding his relationship with Onesimus? What is our Heavenly Father teaching us in these passages regarding reconciliation, forgiveness, and humility? How can multiethnic congregations teach and model a biblical hermeneutic in action? What does it look like?

I agree with my colleague and biblical theologian Rob Wall's reflection upon the function and role of Scripture: "A good interpretation must engage all these sources with prayerful attentiveness to teach Scripture under the Spirit's discretion and by the church's confession to teach, to reprove, to correct, and to train God's people for the ministry of reconciliation."[1] Let us ask questions and interpret scripture.

Why did Paul engage with Philemon? How did Paul engage with Philemon regarding Onesimus? What disputes needed resolution? How did Paul address the issues at hand? These three men had three different cultural contexts, determinations, and perspectives of God's agenda. How did they reconcile their differences? Who led them down the correct path? Why did the issue need attention? The way we interpret and manage leadership is influenced by our cultural context, the Holy Spirit, biblical truth, social resolve, and systems of interacting with others. We are shaped, conditioned, and developed from within our personal preferences.

The other day I went to a colleague of mine and asked for counsel regarding a decision that was set before me. His response: "Whatever you do, make sure God is glorified." I thought that was good counsel. But, as I reflected more about the response, I thought that he took the easy way out because he did not ask questions about specific details of my inquiry. Details are important to God. For the Christian, God must be glorified and magnified in the details. Anyone or anything can glorify God. To magnify God is to go through a process of intentionally making God larger than what is presently seen. God needs to be seen in the details of our processing and working through ideas. We need to make God larger than our situations. How is that done? I believe when we practice acts of justice, mercy, and reconciliation, God is magnified. When we practice giving and relinquishing our personal agendas, goods, preferences, and positions of authority, God is seen in a larger way in that situation.

That is what happened between Philemon and Onesimus. The greater became the least and the least became greater. Thusly, God looked larger than the cultural context of their situations. God's agenda trumped their cultural preferences. God was glorified by becoming magnified. Paul worked on specific details with Philemon regarding what the culture says *do* and yet, more importantly, God says *go*. Yes, the culture says *just do it*; it's your thing, do what you want to do. But, God says, go because when you go, it is implied that you will do something. When we go, we release. We give up. We turn over our will. We leave something behind. This type of *'going'* points to a selfless agenda. Will that something you do take God's agenda to a higher place or greater plain because of your going? Within this context, that is the difference between glorifying God and magnifying God. To truly glorify God, one must magnify Him. Paul said to Philemon, if you forgive and reconcile with Onesimus, God's will is honored, magnified, and glorified. God will be able to raise Onesimus to place of leadership and honor to serve God's great purposes. When dominant culture is willing to submit and lift up non-dominant culture to serve God's greater purposes, God is magnified and glorified. But it is difficult to accomplish God's work when our preferences get in the way.

Simply put, we let our agenda get in God's way. That is what happened to Pharaoh with the Children of Israel. Pharaoh would not let God's people go. Ultimately, Miriam sings to God's glory regarding how Pharaoh and his army had drowned in the Red Sea. God was glorified through Pharaoh's selfish decisions, but God was not necessarily magnified with Pharaoh's differences and preferences, which influenced Pharaoh's decisions. God was magnified in Israel's song of testimony (Ex. 15). The homogeneous mixture of our leadership decisions might glorify God. But those decisions that are influenced by our preferential constructs might not necessarily magnify God. The consequences of some of our decisions do not look like God's diverse multicultural kingdom. When God's people reflect, lift up, magnify, and point to Jesus Christ as our head and God's church as the diverse hands and feet of Jesus Christ, God's holy people are worshipping God in spirit and in truth. This worship is reflected in diversity amongst the people.

Diverse worship gatherings are biblically sound. Diverse church leadership is biblically sound. It makes sense because God's church is diverse and holy. Where there is no leadership, diversity in the preaching of the Word of God, singing, directing the choir, serving on praise teams and in the band, there will be no diversity in the pew. Who we see in the pew should be the nations, tribes, different tongues and people loving each other and worshipping God. We should see diversity in the leadership overseeing the congregation as well. On one hand, for some people it might be difficult to see God's diversity when they do not see it on Sunday morning. On the other hand, some people might be very content with a homogenous mixture within their worship gatherings. But take note, the world is watching us.

Is it possible that the world does a better job with multiethnic and diversity gatherings than the North American church? As for the world's cultural liturgies, such as sporting events, entertainment assemblies, and even within some of their family gatherings, the notion of lifting up different types of diversity is imperative. For this cause, the world wants to selfishly love and lift up selfish love as acts of boastfulness, pride, and self-centered worship.

Whereas, the church must desire to create liturgies and gatherings that not only counteract worldly liturgies design, but more importantly, show to the world that we are Christians by our love for one another and we are unified in holiness because of Jesus Christ (John 17).

CHAPTER 8

MULTICULTURAL LEADERSHIP IN YOUR CHURCH

Growing multicultural leadership within your congregation proclaims hope and feeds a desire for becoming more like Jesus Christ! This desire needs to be fresh and new daily—like the daily bread idea Jesus teaches us in the passage regarding discipleship—the Lord's Prayer. Now the Lord's Prayer is familiar to us. And the danger with familiarity is that it can give rise to spiritual apathy. When one becomes so familiar with the Christian life that there is no need for deeper reflection than the status quo and usual piety, then the spiritual formation that one desired in the first place becomes null and void. In essence, the deeper we grow in Christ, the greater and deeper the suffering, sacrifice, and the loss—but moreover, for gaining Christ and the power of the resurrection. And that must be worth it.

Growing practices hold us accountable. This is not necessarily what Christians in North America want to hear. If we are to gain Christ in the fellowship of His suffering, what does that look like? Face it, we even use the terms *my ministry* or *my gifts* when the fact of the matter is that we own nothing but nothingness, and that which is placed before us is given by the wise Creator, and we must take care of that which is God's in the first place. Encouraging and lifting up the next generation of leaders breeds hope. Cherishing others as Christ cherishes us is Holy Spirit driven. For the author and finisher of our faith teaches us to holistically cherish and grow others! God will not fund our empty cherishing. *Oh Lord, hold us closely within your care and, by your grace, hold us accountable to your kingdom's charge to grow greenhouses of hope and human flourishing!* Praise the Lord!

God is interested in growing God's people! God is interested in resurrecting every sector of life for the glorification of God. It is through our relationships with each other and the earth that God accomplishes His task. Hence, we speak, act, and believe differently regarding the goodness of the earth and what is evil in God's sight. Since the intention of the church (ecclesiology) is to heal, we must strive not to hurt each other with evil intentions.

The challenge of the church is a matter of *intentions*—to seek peace, to do that which is good in God's sight, and to depart from evil. Tradition is only dangerous when it becomes idolatry. Theologians Howard Snyder and Joel Scandrett highlight and present a more complex rubric for the church's ecology. This is challenging. Might we be able to enhance our faith community's diversity and sensitivity to others by taking on the challenge for vibrant change and mission towards a healthy perspective of the earth and our stewardship of it? Perhaps I address this issue because it is out of the comfort zone for some and right at the center of mission for others. The earth is changing. We are changing. The church should be changing into the body of Christ every day—in a greater way. Perhaps for some, leadership change is difficult to swallow. Multicultural leadership is a challenging notion for some congregations. One might inquire, how do we do that? We do it by transcending beyond our cultural codes and comfort zones.

The notion of transcultural transcendence begins with leadership. If the church's leadership has difficulty working outside of her comfort zone, then predictability and the status quo will be the benchmark of her success. True and truly, successful spiritual leadership requires humility to evolve and transcend above the normative confluences of selfishness and sequestered safety nets. Practicing multicultural care is a *stewardship of multiethnic leadership, which begins with these two principles: (A) multiethnic worship is a covenant commission from God, given first to all humanity and (B) through the resources of God's grace and the stewardship of "the manifold grace of God" that has been given us* (1 Peter 4:10).

Leadership must see the task of multicultural care practice as normative. From the parish to the pew, from the many to the few, our laboring must not be in vain and our testimony must proclaim that we, through God's grace and Holy Spirit, will covenant with God again regarding multiethnic sensibilities. We absolutely do not have any other options.

Jesus' prayer for unity in John 17:21–23 states: "That they all may be one, as thou, Father, art in me, and I in thee, that they also may be one in us;

that the world may believe that thou hast sent me. And the glory which thou gavest me I have given them, that they may be one, even as we are one: I in them and thou in me, that they may be made perfect in one; and that the world may know that thou hast sent me, and hast loved them, as thou hast loved me."

Our worship response to Jesus' prayer is to gather multiculturally and intergenerationally in continuous Christian worship. This song is a continuous testimony to the majesty, character, and eternal glory of God the Father, Son, and Holy Spirit. Our songs are no longer heard as a piece of music in a worship set, but as a continuous unified song of the church, ever resounding and articulating the sound doctrine of unification and worship in spirit and in truth.

Is it necessary to embrace the idea of multi-ethnic worship? Is there a greater sense of God's presence in multiethnic gatherings? Is there a particular power that is present there too? The answer is no. The power is in the Word of God that forms and shapes our thinking and how we worship. When we choose to practice and articulate various Christian worship traditions, genres, styles, languages, preferences, and then fuse them together, we are formally and informally being shaped and formed into the character of Christ. How we worship shapes our character. How we worship should never drive doctrine. Doctrine must drive how we worship. We must be driven to worship Christ soundly. For sound doctrine is about God and the sounds of our worship should be too.

Worship Is about God and Musical Genre Is about People.

If we are not careful, genre, style, and preference can easily become forms of idolatry. Our worship should focus on Father, Son, and Holy Spirit. Whatever the worship musical genre might be, God is looking for the spirit and truth worshippers, those who have pure hearts and clean hands and whose intentions are righteous.

What Is Our Worship Response to God's Very Nature and Existence?

Our worship response is a continuous song sung in many parts, various keys, from symphonic forms to simple binary song forms, to African and Asian sensibilities, to artistic fusions of multiple languages and genres. This is an intentional multiethnic continuous song of the church.

This continuous song is sung in many time zones around the world, many languages, and multiple layers of canonic renderings, juxtaposed in great counterpoint to the counter-culture of Christ, orchestrated with a vast array of instruments that have ranges from highest pitches imagined to the lowest decibels unheard with human hearing. This continuous song is a response to the character of God. In order to participate in the manner of how God wants us to worship Him, we must first remove ourselves from the equation. We must take off our shoes in order to stand on His holy ground.

As our worship gatherings become more multiethnic, the world will see that we are Christians because of the way we worship God and our love for one another. Here are four ways worship leaders can implement multiethnic worship expressions and participate intentionally with the continuous song of the church.

1. Learn new musical styles and worship expressions from other ethnic groups by worshipping with them. Have them teach their songs to your congregation.

2. Change your attitude and perspective about how to worship God. Move from desire to conviction and from conviction to being. Be

the change you want to see, and give God the glory for it!

3. Build a multiethnic, intergenerational worship team by developing, in your personal life, cross-cultural relationships with others. Opposites do find each other attractive.

4. Take an ethnomusicology class at a community college and learn different musical genres of other cultures.

CHAPTER 9

POSTLUDE: THE MUSIC BOX

A postlude is a closing phase or final statement in a piece of music. For our purposes in this context, we will interpret postlude as a challenge to carefully review the *music box*. So then, where do we go from here? According to most churches, leadership is critical! We see in the Bible that great leadership breeds success! How do we press our congregations to embrace a multicultural ecclesiology as normative?

Perhaps we might consider seeing ourselves working with a greater leadership imagination. Every community has its cultural codes. God's cultural code for holiness and wholeness is ultimately our vision, goal, desire, trajectory and destiny. Wholeness and holiness work in tandem. This notion is found in the incarnation of Jesus Christ. God in the flesh is fully divine and fully human. God in the flesh is amongst us, living, being, and growing our community. Is it possible to desire something that, on your own, you do not have the capacity to ascertain or comprehend? Yes.

Thirty years ago I decided to leave the wonderful, sheltered life—preacher's kid syndrome, Detroit, Michigan—and take a risk to pursue a degree in jazz composition and arranging at the University of Massachusetts at Amherst. At that time, I was twenty-three years old, and my heart and mind were open to new discoveries. Being a church musician and having very limited experience in jazz, I decided that the process and art of improvisation was something that I wanted to explore. I made a decision to explore. Knowing full well that my parents were not interested in the idea of their son majoring in jazz, I decided to have a go at it. I was a terrible improviser. Within the context of composing in the Western European traditions and gospel music sensibilities, I could be very creative. But I did not play jazz well. To improvise well in a jazz context meant that I had to explore its tradition, the context of that musical language, and its cultural codes. I had to immerse myself within that particular context. I had to live in that community to develop the skills and language for playing jazz.

In order to enlarge your capacity for multi-ethnic worship arts, you must consider being a student of that particular culture. This is *not* easy to do. In essence, one must have a teachable spirit, must develop a spiritual ethic for constancy and diversity, and must perceive the notion of enlarging one's cultural context borders as a moral compass issue. Jesus Christ's command in Matthew 28 is more than an issue of discipleship; it is about our responsibility to expand and enlarge God's kingdom on earth and how we join God in the work of evangelism, creation, flourishing, and doing justice. It is a moral compass issue of wholeness and holiness. Notice the passage: "And Jesus came and spake unto them, saying, all power is given unto me in heaven and in earth. Go ye therefore, and teach all nations, baptizing them in the name of the Father, and of the Son, and of the Holy Ghost: Teaching them to observe all things whatsoever I have commanded you: and lo, I am with you always, even unto the end of the world. Amen" (Matt. 28).

Why do we need to be taught? We need to be taught because we need to learn to be like Jesus Christ. We need to be holy. We cannot learn how to follow Jesus Christ in holiness until we see our own brokenness. When we do not perceive the need to expand our cultural context borders, we fail to see our own brokenness. We go out amongst others because that is what Christ's incarnation did for us. We teach others because Christ taught us. We leave our comfort zone because Christ left His comfort zone. We cannot teach others how to disciple until we have been taught and discipled ourselves. We are taught by Jesus Christ to leave our comfort zone. We can only be fishers of humanity when we cast our spiritual net to that other cultural context of our own rendering. That spiritual net is our giftedness, discipline, and passion for Christ. For it is only under the power of Holy Spirit that we are able to attract, reach out, and draw humanity to the saving grace and power of God the Father.

In order to teach others, one must learn how to teach the other. When we teach others, we learn from others. There is something dynamic that happens in-community when we teach and are being taught. Many times we read this passage with a perspective that when I go to teach others, I am giving them something that I have. Every teacher understands that when you prepare to teach, you are constantly learning and growing and expanding your own understanding of community, its cultural impact, and the epistemology of teaching.

Notice the passage is filled with nuances of being with others. What is very clear is a theology of relationships embedded within the text (Matt. 28). We are not alone. The triune God is not alone. We cannot go and teach in silos. We are commanded to go to the nations. This is not complicated. Simply stated, we must leave our comfort zones. We must embrace the cultural context of others as we embrace our own. Then and only then, will we have something to preach, teach, proclaim, and illustrate. The idea of embracing other cultures is a picture of how God embraces and reconciles humanity. Embracing humanity is good. Hence, we need to preach, teach, sing, and create art that proclaims God's *reconciling* gospel story. And through the Holy Spirit, allowing God's Word through Christian discipleship followed by whatever cultural engagement thereof, to then overtake us in order to shape our perception of Father God's kingdom. Theologian Pedrito Maynard Reid states: "Theology that is contextual recognizes that theological expressions cannot ignore culture and history, nor the varied contemporary thought forms …. Culture is not static. It is always changing, influx and adapting. Just as theology does not make sense unless it is contextualized, worship is not authentic if it is not accommodated to particular eras and particular cultures. Liturgy must take seriously the cultural and ethnic diversity in local and worldwide Christian communities."[1]

Churches choose to engage God through worship and not make a god out of our worship. Genre is about people and worship is about God. In essence, worship genres are boxes. Books are boxes. Songs are boxes. Dramatic plays are boxes. Choirs, worship bands, orchestras, and any conglomeration of people can be interpreted as boxes. One could have a music box, drama box, film box, visual arts box, spoken word box, dance box, or any other artistic rending imaginable, but sometimes that box has nothing to do with God. Whatever is in the boxes or whatever that particular box looks like, Jesus Christ is Lord of it. Christ is Lord of all of those boxes. *To worship outside the music box is to continuously embrace a fresh disposition towards God's perspective of reconciling all things to Jesus Christ.* In order to serve God, we partner with God, desiring to see God's kingdom come to earth as it is in heaven. We explore other culture's music boxes. We import their artistic sounds and biblically sound doctrine into our worship experiences. Simply stated, we decide to choose to cross the comfort zone of preferences and biases. We decide that we will pursue a Holy God with a righteous excellence for creative worship unto God. The end means of our worship is to give our heavenly Father, Jesus Christ, and the Holy Spirit glory. Worshipping outside the music box is a continuous journey of discovery. We refuse to be undisciplined with our comfort zone crossings. We expand our worship articulations. We choose not be complacent with the status quo. We identify our boxes and choose to serve God inside and outside our boxes so as to glorify the Father in heaven. We beckon the Holy Spirit to shape, form, and expand our notions of Christian community. We make a choice to see God's heart for all humanity. All of those boxes from other cultures become beautiful because God reconciles everything—all cultures, all boxes, all people, all art, and all of our worship.

Observe this as type of worshipping outside the music box:

> And they sung a new song, saying, Thou art worthy to take the book, and to open the seals thereof: for thou wast slain, and hast redeemed us to God by thy blood out of every kindred, and tongue, and people, and nation; And hast made us unto our God kings and priests: and we shall reign on the earth.
>
> (Revelation 5:9–10)

Why do we consider doing multiethnic worship arts as ministry? Why are diverse artistic styles of many so important to God? We do multiethnic worship because that is what we will be doing in heaven, so we better get practiced up while here on earth. We practice by doing. We *do* with the notion and goal of growing into that which we need to become. We practice because Holy Scripture instructs us to practice.

This type of practice is made manifest through our love for God and other people. This loving must be practiced. This practicing is one way God brings heaven to earth. This practice is a means by which we as Christians can articulate the love of God as manifested for God's love for all people.

As dark forces in this world and the god of this age who has blinded others creates a diversity that leads to unrighteousness, Christians in this present age should create opportunities to activate and live out a diversity that leads to holiness, wholeness, and hopefulness in the triune God. The practice of loving others is a way we conduct and instantiate multiethnic ministry. We simply must practice being together. On one side of the coin, this multiethnic ministry notion may appear to be too complicated. Do we love and respect other people with a holiness and righteousness that brings God glory? On the flip side of the coin, we can still fail with the notion of arrogance, claiming that we know how to love others and know how to do multiethnic gatherings, but we do not sincerely love others who refuse to embrace God's multiethnic kingdom practices of holiness. Without the power of the everlasting God, we cannot live out multiethnic ministry. It is only through the power of God that we can gather together to be the people of God we are called to be.

At the first ecumenical Council of Nicea, the worldwide church gathered together to decide upon what was necessary to believe. The council was multiethnic. It recognized the relevance and power of a statement of belief—the Nicene Creed. That gathering represented a diverse people and leadership style that understood the power of oneness and unification.

Our desire to be together is important. The challenge here is that most people are content to be in a homogeneous community. It is possible that not all homogeneous communities are able to act on and live out a type of multiethnic or cross-culture ministry. However, wherever there are two or three gathered in God's name, God is there in the midst of them. God is present because God is the focus, and God is to be worshipped. People who have similar cultural contexts do not have to practice sidelining their cultural preferences. The practice of denying one's cultural preference is the practice of denying self. Self-denial puts denying self, first. Denying self situates *taking on the preferences of others* as first. This act of denial affirms the needs and preferences of others as imperative. This act of denial is what Christ did in His incarnation—living out His existence with humanity as fully human and divine. Within Christ's passion in the Garden of Gethsemane, through His death on the cross, to His burial, resurrection, and returning, Christ, who is our *worship leader*, models for us a denying self.

Worshipping outside the music box calls for us to recognize that Jesus Christ is our worship leader. We follow in the footsteps of Jesus Christ. After Jesus Christ's baptism, the Holy Spirit, who anointed Christ, and God the Father who made a declaration to the world by affirming God's presence in the world, we choose to follow Jesus Christ. The triune God was present in the affirmation of Christ. Christians must affirm and confirm our roles and relationships with each other as we are in God's presence, worshipping the triune God. The Trinity models how we must worship God in community with a togetherness that triumphs and trumps any self-proclamation notions of diversity or homogeneous credentials or creeds. The only creed that manifests a God-centeredness is that which gathers all nations and kindred, tongue, and people.

This holy, reverent, diverse living in community reflects God's love, God's hope, God's healing power, God's sovereignty, and God's kingdom on earth as it is in heaven. It fully illustrates, impacts, and relates us to each other and moreover, to our heavenly Father's will. "And hast made us unto our God kings and priests: and we shall reign on the earth" (Rev. 5: 10). Since this is to happen eschatologically within God's kingdom in the age to come, we better practice up and learn how to balance our leadership style with others. Relinquishing control of our music boxes is an act of embracing

God's diverse innovation that our holy heavenly Father has given to the world. At the very core, worshipping outside the music box is this notion of *allowing Jesus Christ to be our pastoral worship leader and the Holy Spirit to be our teacher.* At some point we must make a choice to let God lead us. We make a choice to allow God to gather us together in holy unity. God's leadership design is not for us to control God, but to reign with God. God draws our holy, diverse, multiethnic leadership into the heavenly Father's agenda. God *reins* us in so that we can *reign* with Him—together as a multiethnic body of believers who have made the decision to worship God outside of their music boxes.

BIBLIOGRAPHY

Baker, Dori Grinenko (ed.). *Greenhouses of Hope: Congregations Growing Young Leaders Who Will Change The World.* Hernon, VA: Alban Institute, 2010.

Berry, Wendell. *Jayber Crow.* Washington, DC: Counterpoint. 2001.

Bonhoeffer, Dietrich, and Eberhard Bethge. *Christ the Center.* New York, NY: Harper One, 1960.

Cone, James. *God of the Oppressed.* Marynoll, NY: Orbis Books, 1997.

Guthrie, Shirley C. *Christian Doctrine.* Louisville, KY: Westminster/J. Knox, 1994.

Maynard-Reid, Pedrito U. *Diverse Worship: African-American, Caribbean & Hispanic Perspectives.* Downers Grove, IL: InterVarsity Press, 2000.

Moltmann, Jürgen. *The Coming of God – Christian Eschatology*. Minneapolis, MN: Fortress Press, 2004.

Peterson, Eugene. *Reversed Thunder: The Revelation of John & The Praying Imagination*. San Francisco, CA: Harper Collins, 1988.

Pinnock, Clark H. *Flame of Love: A Theology of the Holy Spirit*. Downers Grove, IL: InterVarsity Press, 1996.

Porter, Stanley E., and Beth M. Stovell. *Biblical Hermeneutics Five Views*. Downers Grove, IL: IVP Academic, 2012.

Stone, Bryan P. *A Reader in Ecclesiology*. Burlington, VT: Ashgate Publishing, 2012.

Synder, Howard A. *Salvation Means Creation Healed*. Eugene, OR: Cascade Books, 2011.

Tanner, Kathryn. *Christ the Key*. Cambridge, England: Cambridge, UK, 2010.

Webber, Robert. *Worship Is a Verb: Eight Principles for Transforming Worship*. Peabody, MA: Hendrickson, 1995.

ENDNOTES

Chapter 2

1. Cone, *God of the Oppressed*, 29–30.
2. Ibid., 35.
3. Stone, *A Reader in Ecclesiology*, 212.
4. Ibid., 213.
5. Ibid.
6. Ibid., 214.
7. Ibid., 213.

Chapter 3

1. Webber, *Worship is a Verb*.
2. Guthrie, *Christian Doctrine*, 163.
3. Ibid.

Chapter 4

1. Attributed to St. Theophan the Recluse.
2. Pinnock, *Flame of Love*, 150.
3. Ibid., 152.
4. Ibid., 157.
5. Ibid., 158.
6. Ibid., 160.
7. Ibid., 187.
8. Ibid., 190.
9. Ibid., 192.
10. Ibid., 218.
11. Ibid., 247.
12. Ibid., 80.
13. Ibid.
14. Ibid., 81.
15. Ibid., 81–82.
16. Dr. Jeff Keuss, Lecture Notes, Seattle Pacific University, April, 2014.
17. Ibid.
18. Pinnock, 85.
19. Ibid, 86.
20. Ibid, 92.
21. Tanner, *Christ the Key*, 274.
22. Pinnock, 83.
23. Ibid., Keuss.
24. Baker, *Greenhouses of Hope*, 16–17.

Chapter 5

1. Cone, 125.
2. Tanner, *Christ the Key*, 142.
3. Ibid., 164.
4. Cone, 126.
5. Tanner, 143.
6. Dr. Brian Bantum, Lecture Notes, Seattle Pacific University, February 6, 2014.
7. Ibid., Tanner, 140.
8. Ibid., 160.

Chapter 6

1. Bonhoeffer, *Christ the Center*, 65.
2. Tanner, *Christ the Key*, 10.

Chapter 7

1. Dr. Rob Wall, Lecture Notes, Seattle Pacific University.

Chapter 9

1. Maynard-Reid, *Diverse Worship*, 44–45.

CONTACT INFORMATION

To order additional copies of this book, please visit
www.redemption-press.com.
Also available on Amazon.com and BarnesandNoble.com
Or by calling toll free 1-844-2REDEEM.